TESTIMONIES, MIRACLES & BREAK

Your Test & Trials Will Become Your Testimony to Encourage Others…

Our God is an Awesome God!

Introduction

January 13, 2021

No matter what is going on in your life, if you trust God and Walk in Faith, everything will work out. I wanted to write this book to encourage others especially my family and friends. Life is going to happen…Trials and Tribulations are going to come…You have to be strong spiritually to stand. Being strong spiritually to stand only comes through our personal relationship with God through Jesus Christ of Nazareth. We have to know deep down in our spirit, soul, heart…our being…without a shadow of doubt that God loves us and everything will work out for our good and for His Glory… (Romans 8:28)

Looking back over the years from when I was a child, a teenager, a young adult, my child bearing years, adulthood and now going into my senior years (Praise God, I am 53), I can see how God had His Hands on me. There were so many instances where I could have lost my mind/gone crazy, or actually left here prematurely in car accidents, etc…But God kept me. There was always Divine Intervention in some way. I almost can't explain it, but me being more spiritual now - I know it was my Angels or some type of Divine Intervention that saved me. To God be the Glory! (I now confess Psalm 91 almost daily over myself and others - Protection, etc)

Maybe because of what I've been through in life…all the trials and tribulations, all I can do is keep trusting God. I have to keep walking by faith. In reality if I looked at some of my circumstances, I would go crazy if I didn't trust the Lord. The only way that I've been able to do that (increase my faith) is by praying; meditating / studying the Word of God and applying it to my life; Worshiping God; Confessing and Decreeing; Intercessory Prayer (praying for others) and actually seeing God work in their lives which is such a blessing; and being a giver. When I say being a giver, I am not just talking about money. I am talking about volunteering, encouraging individuals however you are lead to. I also try to stay optimistic even in the midst of a storm. I am only able to do that because I have made up in my mind to trust God no matter what. Even though I have my moments of uncertainties, I don't stay there. I now know what to do to get myself out of those modes. I pray you can get to that point in your life as well. You will have less stress and more peace in your life…His Peace. (Philippians 4:7)

Whoever reads this book, I pray Numbers 6:24-26 over your life. The Lord bless thee, and keep thee: The Lord makes his face shine upon thee, and be gracious unto thee: The Lord lift up his countenance upon thee, and give thee peace.

Mica Woods

This Book is Dedicated to My Brand New
Beautiful Granddaughter
Kamiyah
*and all of my Grandchildren to come

My Children,
Timeca, Brandon & Brian

My Beautiful Mom,
Ms. Charlotte

My Wonderful Supportive Husband,
Tony

My Siblings,
Reginald, Reynard, Russell & Phillip

All My Nieces, Nephews, Cousins and
other Relatives and Friends

I Love and Appreciate each and every one of you.
All of you have touched my life in some way.
May God Continue to Bless Everyone

TABLE OF CONTENTS

1. Healing / Deliverance 4

II. Protection 11

III. Provision 15

IV. Breakthroughs 20

V. Resources 26
   (Hotline #'s, Prayers, etc.)

I. Healing

I had experienced praying and watching how God worked different situations out in my life. Many of those situations, I prayed in faith and tried my best to trust God. Usually as long as I stayed positive, things worked out. During those times, I also experienced when I allowed confusion and stress to be a part of my life, how things didn't work out. This was mainly due to my anxiety or just wanting to do things my way. Either was, I was miserable and decided early on to try and walk by faith most of the time.

~ One **Healing Miracle** that I experienced is when my oldest son kept getting a fever when he was about 6 or 7 years old. I was not that spiritual but I knew about faith and prayer. I kept giving him fever medicine but the fever kept coming back. This happened at least 3x. I think I had to get up and go to work and was just tired that night. So, when the fever came back again, I was mad. I began praying while holding him…I remember quoting scriptures about healing …by Jesus Stripes He is Healed, etc. - All I can remember is all of a sudden, I felt my son cool off. My hand was on his head and there was literally a coolness that I felt under my hand and his fever left and never came back. It shocked me and I praised God. That's the day that I really started having more faith and most importantly, knew the Power of God!

My mom and youngest son

~ Another incident that happen when my youngest son was about a year old, he got meningitis from a new babysitter. I just started working at a company in a northern suburb so I needed a baby sitter. It was a home daycare. After picking him up from the baby sitter, I noticed that he was not smiling like he normally did. he started looking a little spacey. The next day, he was really looking out of it so I knew something was wrong. I decided to take him to the hospital to find out what was going on. When I took him in, they immediately took him in the back and told me had I waited one more day, he would have been brain dead. I could not believe it…that's why it is important to stay connected to God so you can listen to that still voice (The Holy Spirit) and your motherly instincts. I praise God because although I was not that spiritual back then, I knew something was not right. Praise God today, after a lot of therapy, etc. my youngest son is doing well.

My Youngest Son is now a famous Tattoo Artist and Just an Awesome Artist! Although he has had a few challenges in life as well, he was able to push through…He is so Talented…This is some of his Art…

Mica Woods

~ In 2008, I had to have an hysterectomy because of tumors that could have turned into cancer. Although I had a physical surgery, God also did a work on my mental, emotional and spiritual state. I really believe during this time, I was experiencing some type of nervous breakdown. I had a lot of anxiety and I was not thinking rationally. I was all over the place. The main reason now looking back is that I had loss business income. Someone had under bid me for a transportation contract. I guess I was basing my identity in my business. So, when that failed, I thought I failed. Now looking back, that was crazy thinking because I was very blessed. I was married, had a home, car, etc. There is no reason I should have been in a panic mode. Back then, I was not praying a lot. I was just in what I call, "a rat race." I was trying to become successful in my own strength…busy moving and not going anywhere. After the operation, it took me about 6 months to recover. During that time, I had time to reflect about everything that was going on in my life. Most importantly, I had time to pray and start reading my bible again. After that, I gained my strength physically, mentally, emotionally and most of all spiritually. I guess that operation kind of saved my life. I was able to put things in perspective again.

From what I see and have experienced over the years, a lot of sickness is connected to our mental and emotional state. Looking back, I remember a few individuals who became sick because of a lot of heartaches they were experiencing in their lives. Many of these individuals stopped practicing what I call "self care." They start focusing on their problems instead of our Mighty God, which is what I experienced too. That's when sickness sets in many times. We have to really be careful that no matter what is going on in our lives, we focus on Jesus…the things of God and not our problems. We must remember, Our God is a Mighty God…Bigger than any issue we may be having in life!

My daughter

~ Just recently, the beginning of 2020, my daughter had a cancer scare. The doctor told her they thought they found something and had to do a biopsy. I immediately started praying and fasting for her…that the test would come back negative. I claimed it and just kept fasting a praising God for a good report. To God be the Glory! After about a week, her test came back negative. The doctors just told her they wanted to test her more often since cancer ran in her family on her father's side. I said ok to the doctors wanting to test her from time to time, but any family curses stops here from my side of the family and his side of the family. They will not pass down to my children, grandchildren, great grandchildren, and so forth - In the Name of Jesus Christ of Nazareth.

~ Another Testimony is when God delivered my oldest son from drug addiction which probably led to some type of mental illness. We are not sure if the chemical imbalance came as a result of the drugs and/or other circumstances in his life. He was also never diagnosed. We just knew he was not himself at all. He was not talking right, looking or acting like himself. My oldest son had been through so many heartaches in his life at such an early age. I believe he just had trouble processing everything. Some of what he experienced were as follows: abandonment issues from me…I let him and his brother go and live with their dad after they got in trouble (police picked them up for shoplifting a donut and chips I think) one day after school. Although they kept visiting me every other weekend, not being in the same home could have been devastating to him. He was about 10 yrs old at the time. Now looking back, I realized they needed me more than just on weekends during this time. Their dad had been asking for a couple of years to let them come live with him. After that incident happen, I said ok. I thought it would be good to have boys be around a man more. His dad did the best he could raising him and his brother. However his dad was very strict. I think his dad was trying to prepare him for the world and was just too hard on him and his brother at times. Once my oldest son was in high school, he started rebelling which led to more problems. In the midst of his rebelling, he ended up going to prison and becoming homeless. We tried to assist him most of the time. However during certain points in his life, he was just in a state of rebellion and wanting to do things his way. I believe these and other negative experiences is what led to the sometimes unbearable situations he was experiencing in his life.

In addition to all this, his dad passed suddenly in a tragic accident at work in 2018. This was very difficult for everyone especially for my oldest son. So, maybe the drugs got worse after his dad passing…not sure. All I know is that he needed to go through some personal healing and deliverance from God. I was fasting and praying for him often. I know he needed a Miracle in order to move on in life. There was a lot of turmoil inside of him and I knew he had to find a way to release. Praise God after about 6 months of intensive praying, putting him and the situations on different prayer list, fasting, confessing and decreeing over him, he finally got his breakthrough. I know My God gave him a Miracle Healing. It was like all of a sudden a light clicked in his mind and he surrendered. He is such a strong individual. I knew once he allowed himself to go through personal healing and deliverance, he would be ok. I also know that once this happened and he kept being around his Beautiful Daughter (my first biological Granddaughter), he would want to do better. Praise God, he is. He has been working for a while now. He is such a good dad and husband now to his wonderful wife. She hung in there with him through thick and thin. I know the prayers of the righteous availeth much…Their lives is so blessed now…Peace in their lives and in their home…I am so proud of him. I am proud of all my children.

My Beautiful New Granddaughter - Kamiyah
with Proud Loving Parents - Brandon and Kisha
My oldest son and his beautiful wife

> **James 5:16**
>
> Confess your faults one to another, and pray one for another, that ye may be healed. The effectual fervent prayer of a righteous man availeth much.

*The following is a testimony about my older brother that's a few years older than me. He received a Miracle Healing years ago around 2008. He almost left here but To God be the Glory, with much prayer, he is still here in 2021. This is our mom's testimony about the situation.

~ "God has been truly good to me all my life. I have so many times in many situations that only God can get all the Glory. One time in particular, I remember trying Gods power. My son had overdosed on drugs and his wife didn't want to tell the doctors what she thought he might have had. I told them to check him for everything, and they did. I went home and prayed to God to give him one more chance and before I got back to the hospital he had woke up out of a coma, in his right mind. Only God could have worked so fast and spared his life one more time.

It's wonderful to have a personal relationship with our Lord and Savior Jesus Christ and to know he is a "Right Now God", if we only believe. That old saying is so true, "He might not come when we want him to come, but he is always on time." I thank God everyday for all my children and how he has and is keeping them."

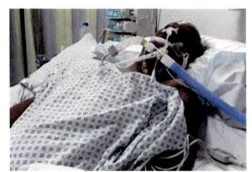 

*These are not photos of my brother, but just a good representation of a Healing Miracle! The Power of God!

II. Protection

Wow, now looking back there have been two car incidents where I literally thought I was a goner…But God! I know there were more car incidents now that I think about it, but these were the main ones.

~ One incident was when I was a young adult, working. I loved to drive fast. I think this is the age where we sometimes think we are invincible. I remember having my brother that worked at the same company or area (downtown Chicago) with me and some friends rushing back to work after going to lunch somewhere. We were running late, so of course I knew I could drive fast. I loved to race my brother and drive fast from time to time so this was right up my alley. However, there was a turn we had to go around to get on the regular expressway. While going into the turn, my car went up on two wheels on the side, screeching…All I can remember is holding on to the wheel tight not knowing what would happen next. But To God Be the Glory, the car came back down and I kept going…slowing down…heart racing and thanking God. I am sure, everyone who was with me in that car that day got out with a different view on life and God. We survived whatever the enemy was trying to do to us that day. To God be the Glory! Thank You Lord for My Angels!

~ Another incident I had while driving. I believe this was during my child bearing years. I was on Lakeshore Drive probably on my way up to visit my oldest brother that lived up north at the time. I had just got on the expressway heading north merging into traffic. All of a sudden a car was coming extremely fast behind me. I think this person was trying to merge on and move into the other lane too fast. In any case, he had to be going at least 50 miles per hour right behind me. I kept honking the horn hoping that he would look up so he would not rear end me going that fast. There was a person in front of me so I could not speed up. In a split second, the person finally looked up and almost had an accident turning into the other lane after he saw he was about to hit me. You talk about Praising God…Although I was shaking like crazy, I knew my Angels had saved me yet again. Divine Intervention. Yes Lord!

~ I do a lot of community outreach especially working with youth. One day while leaving a youth activity, I ended up driving through an actual shoot out. Mind you because I work with youth of all ages, I am usually always dropping youth off. Praise God, this particular early evening, I did not have to drop off any youth. I was actually on my way to visit my mom I believe. In any case, this is what happen.

While driving down 16th Street near Keeler in Chicago, all of a sudden I just head bullets that sounded like they were right at the window of my car. There were all type of cars flying pass me almost running into my car fleeing from the gun fire which is exactly what I started doing. I just drove as fast as I could and kind of ducking a little as I was driving. It almost felt like whoever was shooting was shooting at me. I was screaming "Jesus, Jesus," and driving as fast as I could to get away. When I finally go far enough where I didn't hear anymore shots or see cars driving in all directions, I just cried and thanked the Lord for sparing my life yet again. I was shaking terribly. After I calmed down hours later, I realized that the enemy is not playing. He wants to kill us. The scripture John 10:10 became even more real to me this day.

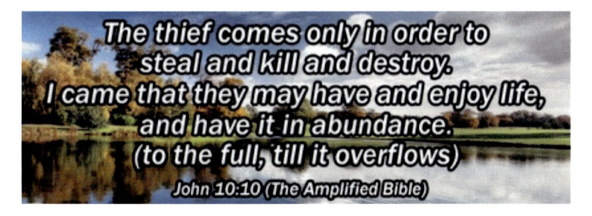

~ An incident that just happen in March of 2021 where I know God used my special needs brother to get me out of harms way was another shoot out that I could have gotten caught up in. Here is what happen.

I had spent the weekend over my moms babysitting with her. It was on a Sunday and my brother and my son were picking up the children. My plan was to take my brother that special needs shopping before I went home but I was not in a hurry to take him shopping. I had even briefly thought about taking a short nap and then take him shopping. In any case, he kept calling me every 15 minutes to ask if I was still taking him. I was use to him calling me every 2 or 3 hours for something.

That's just the way he is. In any case, I decided to go ahead and take him shopping. I was actually getting kind of aggravated. I knew he really just wanted to get out the house. It was about 4:30 pm when I left my moms house. After I took him shopping, I called my mom to find out if she needed anything before I went home. She started telling me that within an hour after I left, there was a shoot out down the street where I park on the side of her building. She told me the police were everywhere - picking up the shell casings, etc. - how even one person that got shot tried to drive himself to the hospital. Wow, this was crazy.

When I really stopped to think about what really just happen and how God protected me yet again, I could not stop praising Him. God can use anyone at any time. God used my special needs brother to bother me every 15 minutes to get me out of harms way.

I don't take anything for granted today. I stay prayerful. I was taught that our Angels hearken to the Word of God. I knew if nothing else, I could confess and pray the Word of God over myself, my children, family and friends, different circumstances and everything would be alright. Also, once you really start reading, studying and meditating on the Word of God, it's like your faith starts to increase more. It's like a knowing you have in your spirit that you will be ok no matter what is going on around you. The scriptures you meditate on really start getting in your spirit. When something happens in your life, you can quote a scripture to give you strength, or do spiritual warfare when needed. Just knowing that I have Almighty God on my side gives me His Peace today. It was not always like that but Praise God today, I strive to keep His Peace in my life. If people or situations arise in my life to disrupt the Peace I have, I immediately deal with it with the Word of God and Prayer.

Now a days, I also try and stay with an attitude of Gratefulness and thanking God for everything…food, shelter, etc. One reason I do this is because at certain points in my life in the past, I would run low on food and God would show up. There was also a time in my life that I was homeless but God kept me. So, I don't take anything for granted.

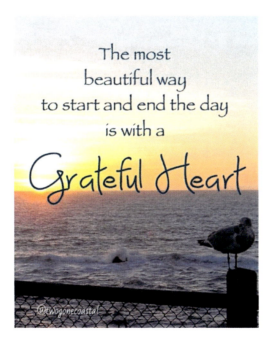

III. Provision

~ Once when my children were young, I think I only had two children then, I had just moved into my own apartment. I had just left my Timmie and was happy to finally have my own place. However, in this particular apartment, I had to pay rent, light and a gas bill. Even though Timmie paid child support and I worked, that still was not enough. Sometimes, my food would get low and I would wonder how I was going to feed my children until I got paid again. To God be the Glory, many times after I would look in the pantry and start putting things together, I would have more than enough food on the table. Now looking back, that was a Miracle Provision from God too.

~ Then there were times when I would be low on food, my mom would pop up with a box of food. I would just cry and thank God. I think back then I walked in pride and had not told anyone I was low on food… how did she know? Looking back now, God was taking care of my children and I even back then… I know that is why I love taking food to families especially single parents. I know from personal experience how difficult it can be at times.

Provision & Miracles Continued…
Surviving Homelessness

~ I literally became homeless in 2002. Even now, when I tell people, they can't believe it. I was homeless with a job, an office, a car and had money in my pocket. This is what happen. I talked to my mom and wanted to buy a family building.

My mom agreed. What we were both paying in rent could be a mortgage. So, when my lease was up, I did not renew it. We decided that I would move in with her, work on our credit and save for our family building. Unfortunately, when I moved in with my mom, about 3 months later, her landlord decides to sell the property. So, everyone in the 2 flat had to move. I was devastated. I was also mad that my mom didn't want to stick to our plan. She stated that she did not have enough privacy with her longtime male friend. Wow, what would I do now. Thankfully, my children did not have to experience being homeless with me. They were able to stay with Timmie's family.

I could not believe this was happening to me. I am so glad I had a car. I slept in my car often. I also had an office. I was able to sleep and wash up there. Occasionally I would stop by my moms and shower over there. But that was a very difficult time for me. God kept me safe while going through being homeless. Eventually a good friend of mine asked me where I was living. I hesitantly cried and told her my situation. She insisted that I come and sleep on her couch. At least I would be safe, could shower and make another plan. I tried to get another apartment, but my credit was not good and it was just a difficult time for me. In trying to make another plan, I ended up meeting my husband. He was the property manager at the building where my friend lived. Even though I would come in late and leave out early, he eventually saw me. I was not suppose to be living there with her because she lived in a subsidized apartment. Once he saw me, he began inquiring about me. He eventually asked me out to lunch. Although dating was the last thing on my mind, I eventually went to lunch with him…long story short, we have been married for 17 years now. I often wonder if the Lord had to slow me down so I could meet my husband. In any case, I am grateful that things worked out. During my homeless experience, I could have gotten killed, went insane, etc. But God kept me through it all. Yes, I cried out to God a lot during that time…I could not understand what was happening in my life. But I kept confessing Romans 8:28…"All things work together for good to them that love the Lord." I had to walk in faith…that's the only thing I had…And everything did work out. To God be the Glory!

My wonderful husband

~ Another provision where I saw the hand of God is in the Not For Profit I started in honor of my maternal grandmother (Mildred Franks - The Mildred Franks Foundation). We were waiting on a donation for toys for our Christmas Event. We were kind of use to getting our toys late from this particular organization. However, this year it was getting later and later. When we did inquire, we were told that they ran out of toys and that we would not be receiving anything. We found out later that this organization had assigned someone else other than the person that normally distributes toys to be over the program this particular year. We were devastated. We had parents / families calling us like crazy. So, we started writing letters, emailing any entity that we thought might give us toys. At the last minute, right before our Christmas Event, we started receiving responses. To God be the Glory. That year we ended up with more than enough toys to serve our families and the community. Since then, our donations have been growing by leaps and bounds to the point that we now donate to other organizations. We now serve almost 10x as many children through our program. I know that is a direct result of us trusting God and Walking by Faith. God is so Awesome! Also, as you develop your personal relationship with God, it's like you walk in more Favor in every area of your life. So, I am really excited about the things of God. Just knowing that I have a Mighty God on my side means the world to me.

Some of the Toys donated from the previous year at the last minute
To God be the Glory!

Now, Look at what God did the Next Year! All the boxes in the back and front were full of Toys! That's the kind of God we serve!

IV. Breakthroughs

My Daughter

~ Another testimony is when my daughter bought her home. She was trying to originally go through a program to get all the incentives etc. as being a first time home buyer. After about a year, that process was not working. They kept telling her she needed all these documents, etc. and giving her follow up appointments months off. It was a disaster. If you know my daughter, after a while she will find another way to get things done which is what she did. I remember all the obstacles along the way of my daughter purchasing her home. At times, she would get so discouraged. I would immediately pray for her and go on a fast many times to keep her encouraged. Eventually, she closed on a beautiful 3 bedroom home. We praised God and knew that He had worked a Miracle on her behalf to get that house. To God be the Glory! She is definitely an example of what hard work and perseverance will do…not to mention the main thing…Trusting God and truly Walking by Faith!

*Not her exact home, but a great representation

Grieving

~ Wow, a breakthrough in grieving. Yes, grieving became so real to be when my Timmie passed. It was like I entered into another world that was just unbearable at times. It's like in a second, my world changed completely and I had no say in the matter. Our children were going crazy it seemed…everyone was grieving hard…family and friends. This was mainly because the accident at work was all of a sudden. The accident was on a Monday and he passed that Saturday. This was totally unexpected. Everyone was just in disbelief for a while and probably still to this day…almost 3 years later. It is still difficult even though today, I have learned how to process the grief better.

I tried to learn about the different stages of grief. This was because I wanted to know about what I was experiencing and maybe get some help on how to alleviate some of this pain. I tried to journal…I actually wrote a book (My Healing Journey: Facing Grief Head On") …I created an online memorial page for him (never-gone.com / Timmie Jefferson). That helped some but nothing really worked until I cried out to God. That was even a process but I could feel myself getting stronger and feeling like I can get through this grieving process with God's help. After almost two years, I can say that although I have my moments, I have accepted that he is no longer here physically. I know he will always be alive in my heart. I also have memories. What really helped is that I know he had a relationship with God. He was not in any type of pain anymore, and he is ok. I am also grateful that after about 3 years now, his children are starting to handle the situation a little better. To God be the Glory!

> LORD, I bring to You my burden because You know my situation. I cannot make it without You. Please comfort my heart, give me strength and help me carry on. Amen

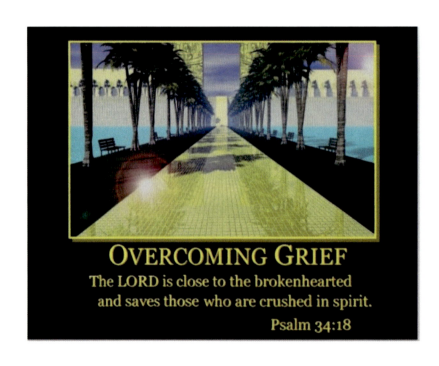

OVERCOMING GRIEF
The LORD is close to the brokenhearted and saves those who are crushed in spirit.
Psalm 34:18

Please if you are grieving, find a way to let it out in a healthy way. Whether you journal, honor the person in some way or just join a support group, it helps. Holding it in will only keep you stagnated in the sometimes unbearable pain of grief. Once you acknowledge the pain, release and accept the situation, you eventually start feeling better. When I say feeling better, I really mean learning to live with your new reality of that special person not being her any longer physically. You may always have those moments, but you don't stay there. You may cry for a little bit but you are able to pull yourself back together with God's help. You never really get over it. You kind of just learn how to live with it in a healthier way. As long as you have your memories, they are still alive in your heart, etc. It may be very difficult at first to allow yourself to go through the grieving process, but with God's help, you can do it. You will be ok and it's worth it for your own well being…your sanity.

In this life, please try and stay with an attitude of Gratefulness and being thankful even for the little things in life. There are so many uncertainties in our world today that can affect our lives in a negative way. But as long as we stay close to God, everything will work out. I had to learn this the hard way through personal experience. Hopefully you won't. You will start developing your personal relationship with God now. So, when difficult times come, you will have an anchor…you will have become strong in the Lord…standing on the Word of God and Walking by Faith…knowing that Our God is Bigger than any issue / problem you may face in life.

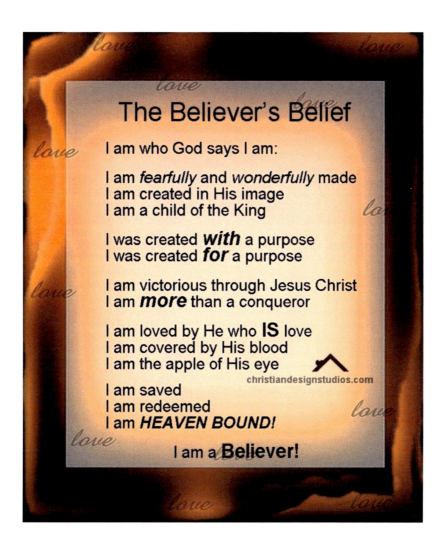

Again, I pray Numbers 6:24-26 over your life.

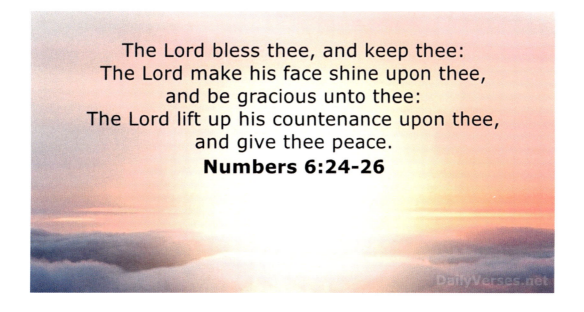

V. Resources

~ Prayers and Other Inspirations:

Salvation Prayer

"Lord Jesus, I believe You are the Son of God and You died for me. Please come into my heart and be my Lord & Savior. I ask you forgive me for all my sins & cleanse me with Your precious blood. Take control of every area of my life from this moment on.

Jesus, fill me with your Holy Spirit & empower me to be used for Your glory.

I will serve You, love You, and obey You all the days of my life. Empower me to make a difference in the lives of others as I share the Good News of Your wonderful gift of salvation. Father, thank you for making me Your child. In Jesus' Holy Name, AMEN!!!"

Our Father, who art in Heaven, hallowed be thy name.
Thy Kingdom come, thy will be done
on earth as it is in Heaven.
Give us this day our daily bread
and forgive us our trespasses
as we forgive those who trespass against us.
And lead us not into temptation,
but delivery us from evil.
For thine is the Kingdom, and the power, and the glory
forever and ever. Amen

Theology 101 – Deeper Connection

Compounds Names

NAME:	SCRIPTURE:	MEANING:
Jehovah-Jireh	Genesis 22:14	The LORD will provide
Jehovah-Rapha	Exodus 15:26	The LORD that heals
Jehovah-Nissi	Exodus 17:15	The LORD our victory
Jehovah-M'Kaddesh	Exodus 31:13	The LORD that sanctifies
Jehovah-Shalom	Judges 6:24	The LORD our peace
Jehovah-Saboath	I Samuel 1:3	The LORD of Hosts
Jehovah-Elyon	Psalm 7:17	The LORD most high
Jehovah-Raah	Psalm 23:1	The LORD my Shepherd
Jehovah-Hoseenu	Psalm 95:6	The LORD our maker
Jehovah-Tsidkenu	Jeremiah 23:6	The LORD our righteousness
Jehovah-Shammah	Ezekiel 48:35	The LORD is Present

Connecting Point Community

Names of God
THE OLD TESTAMENT

El Shaddai	Lord God Almighty
El Elyon	The Most High God
Adonai	Lord, Master
Yahweh	Lord, Jehovah
Jehovah Nissi	The Lord My Banner
Jehovah-Raah	The Lord My Shepherd
Jehovah Rapha	The Lord That Heals
Jehovah Shammah	The Lord Is There
Jehovah Tsidkenu	The Lord Our Righteousness
Jehovah Mekoddishkem	The Lord Who Sanctifies You
El Olam	The Everlasting God
Elohim	God
Qanna	Jealous
Jehovah Jireh	The Lord Will Provide
Jehovah Shalom	The Lord Is Peace
Jehovah Sabaoth	The Lord of Hosts

Ephesians 6:10-18a

- 10 Finally, my brethren, be strong in the Lord, and in the power of his might. 11 Put on the whole armour of God, that ye may be able to stand against the wiles of the devil. 12 For we wrestle not against flesh and blood, but against principalities, against powers, against the rulers of the darkness of this world, against spiritual wickedness in high *places*. 13 Wherefore take unto you the whole armour of God, that ye may be able to withstand in the evil day, and having done all, to stand.

The *Lord* is my shepherd; I shall not want.
He makes me to lie down in green pastures;
He leads me beside still waters. He restores my soul;
He leads me in the paths of righteousness, for His name's sake.

Yea, though I walk through the valley of the shadow of death, I will fear no evil; for You are with me; Your rod and Your staff, they comfort me.

You prepare a table before me in the presence of my enemies; You anoint my head with oil; My cup runs over. Surely goodness and mercy shall follow me all the days of my life; and I will dwell in the house of the Lord forever.

PsalmsQuotes.com

Psalm 23

Psalm 91

He that dwelleth in the secret place of the most High shall abide under the shadow of the Almighty. I will say of the LORD, He is my refuge and my fortress: my God; in him will I trust. Surely he shall deliver thee from the snare of the fowler, and from the noisome pestilence. He shall cover thee with his feathers, and under his wings shalt thou trust: his truth shall be thy shield and buckler.

Thou shalt not be afraid for the terror by night; nor for the arrow that flieth by day; Nor for the pestilence that walketh in darkness; nor for the destruction that wasteth at noonday. A thousand shall fall at thy side, and ten thousand at thy right hand; but it shall not come nigh thee. Only with thine eyes shalt thou behold and see the reward of the wicked. Because thou hast made the LORD, which is my refuge, even the most High, thy habitation; There shall no evil befall thee, neither shall any plague come nigh thy dwelling.

For he shall give his angels charge over thee, to keep thee in all thy ways. They shall bear thee up in their hands, lest thou dash thy foot against a stone. Thou shalt tread upon the lion and adder: the young lion and the dragon shalt thou trample under feet.

Because he hath set his love upon me, therefore will I deliver him: I will set him on high, because he hath known my name. He shall call upon me, and I will answer him: I will be with him in trouble; I will deliver him, and honour him. With long life will I satisfy him, and shew him my salvation.

2 Chronicles 7:14

If my people, which are called by my name,
shall humble themselves,
and pray, and seek my face,
and turn from their wicked ways;
then will I hear from heaven,
and will forgive their sin,
and will heal their land.

It doesn't take much to get started if you want to believe in a God of miracles. Just look at Him. Walk with Him. Commune with Him. Read His word. Occupy your thoughts with Him. And suddenly you're a faith person. It's His presence which makes it all possible.

Jamie Buckingham
www.JamieBuckinghamMinistries.com

~ Google 24 Hour Prayer Lines - whichever ones you feel comfortable with, add them as part as your support system.

~ Visit a Christian Bookstore or research on-line different Prayer Books, Study Bibles, etc. to keep yourself encouraged in the Lord.

~ Prayer Books - There are many that have been helpful to me over the years…times when I was so distraught, I couldn't think straight let alone pray…these Prayer Books were helpful…at least I was praying God's Word over the situation or person.

~ Suicide Hotline - 1-800-273-8255

~ Food Bank, etc. Information

~ Homeless Prevention Hotline Numbers:

Homeless/Runaway National Runaway Hotline
800-231-6946

If you are a teenager and are thinking about running away from home, or if you are already living on the streets, call the National Runaway Switchboard. The Switchboard is a toll free, confidential hotline. Dial **1-800-621-4000** or visit the Switchboard's website.

24/7 at 1-800-RUNAWAY (1-800-786-2929)

~ **Other Books Written by Mica Woods:**

"My Healing Journey: Facing Grief Head On"

"My Exciting Life - Memoirs of Mica R. Woods"

Made in the USA
Middletown, DE
26 May 2021